S0-BTZ-269

A RECOVERY OF SELF

THE DEBRIS
OF THE
ENCOUNTER

Terre Ouwehand

RESOURCE PUBLICATIONS, INC. ● San Jose, California

Editorial director: Kenneth Guentert
Production editor: Elizabeth J. Asborno
Editorial assistant: Cathy Blain
Cover design: Ron Niewald
Cover production: Terri Ysseldyke-All
Cover art: Mary Heebner, *Botany #11*, 39½" x 28", 1987,
charcoal on paper

© 1990 Resource Publications, Inc. All rights reserved. For
reprint permission, write:

Reprint Department
Resource Publications, Inc.
160 E. Virginia Street, Suite 290
San Jose, CA 95112-5848

Library of Congress Cataloging in Publication Data
Ouwehand, Terre, 1953-
The debris of the encounter : a recovery of self / Terre
Ouwehand.
p.   cm.
ISBN 0-89390-137-7
1. Christian poetry, American. I. Title.
PS3565.U98D4 1990
811'.54—dc20 89-38700

5 4 3 2 1 / 94 93 92 91 90

White Noise (1987) and *Radu* (1988) first appeared in *Life Times
Magazine*.

The Dark Knight and the Soul first appeared in *Modern Liturgy*
16:4.

To
Leslie and Myrna,
who, from their different directions,
kept nudging me
into the light

Contents

Introduction
What's Going On Here?

What's going on here? I must ask this question—of myself, of friends, colleagues, acquaintances—at least once or twice a day. It has become my anthem. I enter a room and I can hear it—with full musical score—my theme song. Like the opening to the old December Bride TV show.

So. What *is* going on here?

My therapist is the only one who'll *admit* she doesn't know. It doesn't seem like much to be paying for, but it sounds like the Truth. Capital T. And I like that sound.

You see, just getting to the question isn't easy.

For me it began when my cat died and I had a small but definable mental breakdown. Some friends and family recommended that I snap out of it. After all, a cat. But one friend said it didn't matter what I loved; I loved her for that, and I knew I wasn't crazy. But I saw that I had lived much of my life with a debilitating, depressed worldview in which humanity was perhaps a step above microbes—it was obvious animals had more integrity. So I got the therapist anyway.

One day, to both our surprise, I told her I wanted a guru instead. She wanted to know why, and I said because I don't believe in God. But would like to. I'm a pretty hardcore modernist, a rationalist. I trust what I experience through perception, logic. Yet, I find myself wandering into empty churches. I buy recordings of Gregorian Chant! (That is, if no one I know is in the store and if the woman behind the counter doesn't recognize me from the last time I bought some.) I like the art and architecture of God. Maybe I'm a closet Seeker. Anyway, I thought I should check it out, just in case there's something to it.

She took the job. We began referring to my work on myself as a "spiritual quest." We didn't do anything differently, just modified our vocabulary. And I began to meditate.

In the fall of '85, I was persuaded by a friend to attend a weekend retreat curiously titled The Sound of Om. I required industrial-strength persuasion as I thought all such self- actualization, spiritual-woo-woo seminars were slickly packaged loads of carbuncle, or at the very least, a fine and fancy—however temporary—Band-Aid for whatever ails you. But "for some reason" (my friend's quotation marks), I went.

Something broke. Something broke open in me the last day of the experience. It was tangible. Something like thick glass, high in my chest, quietly broke. Suddenly I was crying, and couldn't stop, though I had no idea why I was! (And I am not a crier—it's unbecoming.)

The gathering had been housed in a large, private home across from a mission, which I looked at daily through the garden gates. I packed my things, stowed them in my car, and walked to it. "Thank God" (my quotation marks) there was no one there. As I stepped into the sanctuary, I had the inexplicable but overpowering feeling of *coming home.* I started crying again. I walked toward the altar, lay face down on the cool, stone floor, and felt very, very grateful. For that feeling, I guess.

I became more serious about *checking it out.* I read. I questioned people. I started acquiring a reputation. I'd be introduced to someone and instead of the customary, "And what do you do?" I'd ask, "So, What are your religious beliefs, and what are they based on?" I was the bane of small talk.

Then, in the spring of 1986, I was sitting in the living room of a friend's condominium, which looks out over the city to the ocean. I wasn't looking at the view. I was facing in the opposite direction with my eyes closed, meditating. Suddenly, something happened. A figure appeared before my mind's eye: a long, transparent figure, draped in pale blue robing, suspended in mid- air, palms opened outward. Beneath his feet, but not touching them for he hung gently in pure space, was a small mound of earth and tiny flowers.

My concentrated breathing, which had always been uncomfortable during these meditation practices, became suddenly effortless, rolling in and out of my torso like a wave. I marveled at the figure. Without thinking in words, I wondered what/who it was. Was I making this up? I didn't remember making it up. It certainly didn't seem like something I *would* make up.

Even as I watched, part of me wanted to write it off as something my subconscious conjured up for whatever bizarre reason, yet clinically explainable. But I wasn't doing any analyzing at the time; I was far too intrigued, mesmerized, by the experience itself. So I just stayed with it. Then something even stranger occurred. I saw my own arms reach out in front of me. I watched them touch the opened palms of the figure before me. He clasped my hands and drew me toward him, but as I emerged into my own line of vision, it was a child I saw, perhaps seven or eight years old. They began dancing around the little mound of flowers, and even in my deep state of relaxation I could feel a warm delight flow like a fluid through my body.

I didn't recall it stopping, but abruptly everything was gone and I was gently stretching my neck and slowly opening my eyes. What impressed me most was the spontaneity of the whole thing. Where had such a sequence of images come from, and why? How real it seemed!

"So what's going on with me?" I asked my therapist/guru in a more specific vein. She gave me the term *spontaneous eidetic image,* but not necessarily as an explanation of what was going on. An eidetic image is something you see with the mind's eye. It's like a vision, but inside. Much of what has been recorded throughout the ages as visions were perhaps eidetic imagery. It can be a powerful experience, and until recently we didn't have the psychological understanding to distinguish the two. And we still can't separate either of them with any certainty from hallucination or imagination. Some help.

Well, whatever and from wherever they were, I had more of them throughout that summer. It was a rush like no other, I'll tell you. I became quite enthralled with my blue-gowned visitor and was profoundly touched in ways I cannot even speak of yet. Then it stopped. I mourned the loss of this curious relationship and complained of the

4

dryness of my meditation. (The phenomena returned the autumn of the next year, and again lasted approximately a season.)

Then something really weird happened.

I was making love with a beautiful, sensitive young man, some years my junior. It was our first time together, and we were very open and moved by each other. Suddenly, at less than an appropriate moment, my hands and lips began to vibrate very oddly and quite strongly. Wow, I thought, I'm really turned on! But it increased to what became a truly disconcerting and even uncomfortable state, and I finally had to say something. He was abundantly understanding; he was into metaphysics. He said it was the releasing of an energy block, which our lovemaking had somehow tapped and unleashed. Quite a line, I thought.

To my astonishment, my therapist confirmed his diagnosis. I was "plugged in." Plugged in? To what? To the Energy that pervades and sustains the Universe, she offered. The Energy that Is. That heals. Everybody has it, but not everybody gets plugged in. You can heal with your hands by employing that energy, she ventured, despite my rational frown. Try it. *Try it?* Was *she* crazy? No, she was plugged in. She showed me.

OK.

I tried it, and one of my friends avoided painful disc surgery. Another experienced reduction in size of uterine fibroid cysts. Others reported simply an inexplicable sense of well-being. I didn't understand it. But it worked. Not always so dramatically and sometimes seemingly not at all. But something was definitely going on here. I would try to

meditate while I was doing this laying on of hands
number; I didn't really know if that was what I *should* be
doing, but I figured that it would probably be a good
thing.

One evening when I was working on my friend's back, I
went deeply into a meditative state and I saw him again,
my mysterious figure. He was suspended in navy blue
space with stars all about, and his arms were outstretched,
cross-like. And then I saw his face. It was incredible. I
realized later that I'd never clearly seen his face till then,
that it had always been rather vague, opaque. But now I
was seeing it, and it was so real that it was startling. It
made the rest of the scene, even his outstretched body,
appear less real, like a picture. It was like a picture with a
real face. And it was beautiful in a way that we don't
understand beautiful. Well, I was gone. I don't know what
my friend got from that session, but I got a great deal. I do
remember that afterward we smiled at each other a lot.

I'm a poet. I hadn't been writing much poetry, though, as
I'd been caught up in writing plays and theatre pieces.
Poetry started welling up; all I had to do was put a
notebook under it as it spilled. From late 1986, most
heavily throughout 1987, and into 1988, it poured forth. It
was immediately different from anything I'd written in the
past. Not only was the content radical, but the
composition, the way in which it came, as well. Something
would happen in my subconscious—it was like going
some place. Sometimes I'd read over a poem I was
working on and almost wonder, who wrote this? I had
trouble matching words I knew I'd written to the person I
still thought I was. This is certainly not the kind of thing
that I would write, an incredulous part of me would
declare. It's so (yipes) religious! I felt schizophrenic. It

was eerie. But it was also a profound wonder, and I think I would have been more worried if I hadn't felt *so good.* My creative highs got higher and better. Ecstatic. Sometimes (particularly with "Gale Struck" and "Mass for a New Age") I'd just have to lie down—not from exhaustion, but...rapture? I simply couldn't and didn't want to do anything else. It was better than drugs. It was better than sex. I didn't know what was going on but I was certainly enjoying it, regardless of my puzzlement at what I was producing. If there is a God, perhaps S/He chooses the least likely—the impious, the doubter, the outsider—for His/Her communiques; then no one can blame the bias of the messenger, right?

So. I still don't know what's going on here, but these are my experiences captured in poems and recollected meditations. I use the term *meditation* broadly and to cover several types of experiences. Some of the poems came through almost fully formed during actual periods of focused relaxation that we associate with the practice of meditation. Others were composed in a more conventional way but under the tremendously powerful new inspiration that I have tried to describe. Then there are prose recollections of spontaneous imagery, scenes, those inner visions, which occurred during periods of meditation. And there's one short story, which I "saw" and "heard" while in a meditative state about a character who sure felt familiar, especially during that long hiatus between the first series of images and the second. Although I numbered the writings as they arrived chronologically, such an order no longer seems important; but their numbers often remain as titles.

Those who have written about "mystical" experience throughout history often warn the Seeker not to get caught up in the extraordinary for its own sake—the sensationalism of psychic occurrences—that indeed, it is a pitfall and easily succumbed to. One modern writer characterized them as *debris from an encounter,* that which remains after the "visitor has gone," and though I have no doubt that she intended her readers to hold suspect anything so disdainfully labeled, I had quite a different response. I saw this debris to be like relics—like venerated bones, sacred ground, an image-seared shroud. These too are what remain: the debris of profound encounter between our world and that which is greater than our world—yes, probably between the human and the divine. My provocative experiences are *my* holy relics, my sacred souvenirs from an encounter with something beyond myself, at least as I define myself. Faith, another author suggests, is remembering what you know, and what you know is what happens to you.

This is what I know...

Meditations

God is a River
(meditation 9)

God is a river
flowing—flowing—eddying
into inlets I chisel in my old stone coat,

seeping into crevices I chip away, and chip away at,
swirling into the little bays I shovel with agony
and angst into the banks of my resistance...

Sometimes
God is a flashflood—
sweeping me from moorings, shouldering me atop
an unexpected rush—flushed and altered by the drama
and the power of the erosion of what I thought
was so...

But mostly
God is a river, working
quietly, subtly,
steadily
at the granite 'round my soul.

A Personal Nativity
(meditation 17)

In eastern reaches of my soul a tiny miracle gestates:
a granule of hope and longing swaddled
like a pearl in the flesh of my discomfort
grows, evolves, smoothes itself,
daily rounding, clothing
in beauty unexpected, unimagined—

This happening is rumored by a curious light
in my head, a brilliant blackness
behind the eyes, a bright darkness
bewildering, quickening my heart to pilgrim
through the night of my own being
to find this unrevealed jewel, this
secret of myself—
         to be barred
from the world's hectic lodgings, by
choice, a happy refugee, glad
to rest in the humble straw, lie down
oxen-dumb and lamb-content
before this wonderous inner thing,
this birthing of belief, this miracle of knowing.

Meditation 10

The universe moved inside me today:

> my breath

> rushed shallow—
> senses fused—

> my heart

> opened like an easeful lover—
> exploded through my body!

And I gasped under the finger of God—

May 1986

A profusion of light! White, golden, beautiful light— all
around me—all I can see. Then, as if I have taken a step
backward, I see a small figure silhouetted against the
colossal backdrop of light. It is a child— but more like a
stick-figure, cartooned. Suddenly out of the light emerges
the silent, pale blue-gowned figure—he picks up the child
and raises her into his arms. He turns to re-enter the light,
and I see the stick-child is a human child, full-fleshed,
blond, content. They disappear into the brilliant light...

Meditation 11

Trees
are God's particular sign posts:
they are always pointing in the right direction.

No matter how many
bends, or twists, or turns
a tree must make, it grows always
toward the light.

If you seek gainful employment—
If you desire a sense of purpose in life—
Be a tree.

White Noise

(meditation 12)

Do you hear it?
The sound of everything and every sound?
The falling of sand, and the piling of stones—
The turning of the world—
The combustion of stars, and the drop, drop, drop of water.
The roar and whisper of the universe!
It is every voice that ever spoke, and speaks.
Every cry and every song. Every sigh, every mumble, every
murmur. Every question and every statement. Every
exclamation! Every laugh and shout and prayer—
It is violins and lawn mowers. Metronomes and hinges.
Bells and braying and chirping and trumpets. Cawing and
hissing. Rustling and lowing, clacking and ticking and
talking and talking and saying and saying and saying. It is
all the words that have ever been, and every unlanguaged
utterance.
It is every sound and the sound of everything.
It is the hum and buzz of being.
It is vibration manifest.
It is energy made breath and blood and chord.

But, listen —

Listen!

Inside. Inside...

Listen!

In the center. Deep, deep, deep in the Center of the sound
of the Sound—

> Is the Silence.
> The Absolute Silence.
> The only silence.

There.
At the very center, inside the sound. There,
God does not speak, but is heard.

July 1986

Casa de Maria Chapel, Santa Barbara

I am looking down into the chapel—from a great height—almost the ceiling, from the front window—the position of the crucifix. Slowly I realize that I am in his arms—and we are both looking out from the cross! The sensory impression of his arms across my upper chest and shoulders is extraordinarily vivid—the smoothness of his skin, the gentle strength of his muscles...

I am suspended effortlessly—as if there is no gravity—he does not have to hold me up, I am weightless—just looking out from his arms...

Good Friday
(meditation 13)

He saw them in the twilight of the thunder's gray passing,
far below, small and scurrying, clustered, clamoring,
like ants, as from an airplane window—saw them
in their minute pride, their tiny, terrible rage,
with their lilliputian hammers and their lilliputian
swords, their lilliputian rocks and spears...

And he forgave them.

He saw the others, too, nearly
indiscernable specks, for he was almost home now—
the ones who would stay, the ones who would cower
and cringe, and pray and wail, and wait till the sky
would close again...

And he forgave them, too.

Meditation on Modern Man

I have felt the tops of trees
fingerng the hem of Eternity...

I have heard God sigh
in the downing of the wind...

I have sensed the immensity of being
in the hulking grace of mountains...

My mind slams. Shut.
Unscientific. Unreliable.

I am a man of mechanisms,
of materials, analysis and industry—
I am king of things!

Love is a luxury—but I am bountiful
in Reason! Plentiful in Proof!
I am the heir of Enlightenment.

Why do I cry in the dark?

Meditation in Notre Dame de Paris
(meditation 14)

Oh, Great Lady,
whose glorious house this is,
perhaps you know me
in this falling close of colored light,
in this soft gloom—for I cannot determine
when or how, but I am a memory here...
a murmur in the stone, a breath upon the glass, a whisper
amongst so many riding the airs that sift and glide and
muzzle along the aisles, lodging in an ancient archway
mooring for times upon a carven head—hung to a lip,
stowed in a cap, until the flap and push of a passer's
breeze set us travelling again, gliding and sifting and
nudging the dust...

Oh, Great Lady, do you know me?
For my skin stirs, my blood begins to chant, my feet
immure in the cool, flat stone as I wade in the gathering
gray, and my hands seek instinctively inside opposing
sleeves, anchoring to a forearm...and all the common
boom of being settles mute and sloughs away...

Oh, Great Lady,
welcome me home—
I am a memory here.

Meditation 7

there is something about
living up high—
where clouds are at eye level—

as if God
might walk in over the terrace,
and it would seem perfectly natural—

or that I
could step off
and be upheld
by thinking the perfect thought...

Divine Dialogue

I'm here, Lord! I'm here!

WHERE?

Behind these closed eyes.

WHY DO YOU NOT COME OUT?

Because I do not know how to see.

SEE ME WITH YOUR EARS. YOU HEAR ME. DON'T YOU?

My mind does not believe such unreliable reports.

SEE ME WITH YOUR HEART. YOU FEEL ME, DON'T YOU?

The heart is sentimental; so easily fooled.

THEN SEE ME WITH YOUR SOUL. YOU HAVE A SOUL, DON'T YOU?

I don't know. I don't know where it is.

IT IS WITH ME. YOU'RE HERE. YOU'RE HERE.

June 1986

I am lying on the floor of a great cathedral—face down— I
feel the cold smoothness of the stone against my cheek, its
unrelenting hardness against my hip bones. I lie there,
very still, for some time... Then, I feel someone or
something lifting me from behind—gently lifting me up
from underneath my shoulders. We begin to ascend—as if
I weighed nothing—Suddenly I can see all around
me—not just forward through my eyes—and I see that I
am being held aloft by an enormous angel—We rise
slowly—as we reach eye-level with the tops of the great
windows we hover—a little ways from the vaulted
ceiling—Then easefully we ascend right through the stone
vaulting and up into clouds...

The Invitation

(meditation 15)

I am an opened window,
I am shutters flung outward,
expectant, a lover waiting—

I am a newly wrenched door, pried
and swung wide—and I am hoping
inside, in the dark, blinking,
sucking anticipation—a square edge
of the world before me:

> Come!
> Fill me!
>
> Strike my soul!
>
> Swell this aching room—
> Burn it white and thick!
>
> Burst me into Being.

Meditation 3

holy spirit,
to you I give
my love for my friend:
it is made of fire.

temper, hammer, mold it,
make it pure—
make it a staff for her to lean on,
make it a sword, a cradle,
a river and a bridge, a sunrise,
a wind and a blanket, a stone,
make it a pillow for her head,
and a roof against the rain.

Gale Struck
(meditation 16)

Blow, Spirit, roar and hush—
rush and flap my soul
like a rug snapped to the breeze!

Gust me as a great wind hurricanes a hill
swooping, trembling oaks, sudden-harvesting
orchards in hails of bud and leaf and pulp!

Burst me from these limbs I've climbed,
from tips of which I strain and reach, on which
I hang and hope—

                hurl me like ripe fruit
to split upon the ground!   To ooze,
radiant-thick, to nourish what patch
of wounded earth lies 'neath me,

to be broken and blessed and tasted by God.

July 1986

I see only my sandaled feet—I am looking down—walking over hilly, barren, desert-like terrain—I reach the crest of a hill-path and see in the distance a crucifixion. I am vaguely troubled, sad, as the realization of what I am seeing breaks over me—I hear my voice say, oh no...quietly... I have the sense of being surprised—caught off guard—that the scene I've chanced upon is unexpected—yet not completely unforeseen—it's the disappointment of realizing one is too late...

August 1986

St. Mary's, Kensington

On a stream of doves—I fly through a dark space in the stained glass—fly through an opening in his side—into darkness that is not fearful but kind and careful—a deep but soft midnight darkness. I can see quite clearly everything around me as I rise above them—streets, cars, houses, neighborhoods—He catches me in mid-flight—I cling to his thin blue robes—We travel upward—as if we trod some stairway in the warm dark sky...

Meditation on the Lord's Prayer

Our Father and Mother who are Heaven
How beautiful are your names,
Your peace be come, your will be done,
So below as it is above...

Give us this day what is needful
And forgive us our unkindnesses
As we forgive those who are unkind toward us,

Keep us strong against temptation
And guide us away from evil,
For you are the Love and the Light and the Glory
Within us all, Amen.

The Introduction

I met Death today—
in soft monastic morning light, on my way
to breakfast among dark cassocks...

I checked my pace, we moved
together, slowly, very
slowly, for Death was in a wheelchair,
click, clack, over the concrete cracks,
click—clack...

Death looked out from gray-ringed eyes,
spoke uneasefully from rusted lips hanging
on a sallow mask—but glad to try, for Death
was only twenty-nine and Death had things to say.
About art. Mathematics. Florence. Poetry, and
looking pretty. She needed clips for her hair.

We ferried toward our futures, toward
smells of eggs, and incense...
At the dining room door, Death raised
a hollow hand jointed at the end of a stiff
stick, sheathed in pale, taut skin,
and waved—

Then Death rolled away, click...
clack...over the concrete cracks.

Salutation

My brother, myself,
my soul's bright reflection!

Mirror of my mind, heart's harbor
gladness-tossed or grieved—

Companion in living's concentric tides,
we move outward from ourselves
eyeing each other safely over the swells—

My sister, myself,
diviner of the best in me!
Where we are two
there surely then is three.

Meditation on Psalm 23

The lord is my shepherd
and my brother and my teacher:

He joins me at the still waters of meditation,
he invites me to lie down in the green meadows
of God's memory...

Though I walk through streets of violence and strife,
I feel only pity and compassion, for he
walks with me—his robe and his hand
steady and comfort me...

He opens my heart in the midst of adversity,
he pours on my mind his peace, and my soul
spills over, it is so full.
Goodness and gladness are mine
whenever I make room for them.
I will share all my days with the lord
and spend them in the house of life.

September 1986

St. Mary's the Virgin, Chipping Norton

The stained glass melts away from the center of the window—as if being burned from the other side—until it is mostly a frame around darkness—in the center of which he stands—suspended in the midnight blue. He stretches a hand toward me—welcoming—or beckoning?

Meditation

5

Awaken
my
hands
to
your
work

And
hear
them
clap
the
joy!

Appraisal

Thank you, Divine Mother,
for the glittering silver spread
of the ocean's expanse,

for the opalescence of the cloud
and pastel streaked sky,

for the jade and amber of the hills,
the jet and agate of the land—

how rich is the day!

And what wealth I amass toiling
only with my eyes.

Radu

Radu sat down to meditate. He postured for his daily
attempt. He did not know if he truly believed. But he did
truly hope. How he hoped! And now he guarded against
his own hope's disappointment. What if it were all a
delusion? A grand illusion that had fooled some of the
world's, some of history's, best? That would be
unbearable, he thought, as he felt his body begin to sink.
It was one thing to be disregarded by one's father, by
one's mother. To be left on a relative's unpainted porch in
the new hours of life. Yes, that was one thing, a hard
thing, to be sure. But to be disregarded by God—because
he didn't exist—to be profoundly fooled, deluded in the
face of the ultimate question—that would be too much.
That would break him, finally. And so he sat down
tentatively each day, daring himself to find the truth.
Challenging his hope. Testing his potential for
disappointment. He sat. He breathed.
In—out—deep—slow—in—out—deep—slow—

He wanted to open himself and purify himself. He
imagined his head splitting and molding itself into a
funnel, and he imagined the most glorious light, all white
and gold, pouring into it from somewhere high above. He
imagined his thoughts, those little pesky flits of thought
that distracted him while he tried to meditate—imagined
them sloughing off his shoulders and back like old scales
and dirty raindrops. And he waited.

He waited for something marvelous. Something extraordinary to happen, to take shape inside his head. He knew of marvels, had experienced them in the past when he was still very new at this practice. He didn't understand them. He didn't know if they came from his own subconscious, if they were hallucinations, fantasies, or evidence of the truth he was looking for. He didn't think he was making them up. They were extraordinary things, holy things, that he would never dream to make up. Most of the time it was a figure, a visitor, at the center of what he saw in his mind's eye—a beautiful red-robed figure with dark hair and a thin dark beard, and sometimes he had his arms outstretched. The figure filled him with such well-being, such fullness—and now he was gone.

Lately his meditations felt dry. The old doubter who lodged in a dark corner inside of him woke from several months of slumber and wagged a finger at him. "It's not real, you idiot," he chided Radu, "just tricks of the mind—there's no such realm and no such beings. God is a concept we create to make ourselves feel better. You're not going to fall for that, are you?" It was hard to stop his ears against the ruthless little voice, and it pained him that he'd lost contact with this mystery, no matter who or what it was.

So he sat, and so he pined and hoped, and tried not to pine and not to hope for that would cloud his concentration and would premeditate whatever happened. He breathed and counted his breaths to quiet his mind. He imagined the ocean—the ocean, he thought, would help settle his concentration. The ocean was deep, and thick and massive and serene.... Suddenly on the very horizon line of the sea, he spied a cross, just planted there on the edge of the ocean. He stared through his mind's eye. To his further surprise, a small moon emerged from behind the cross, from beneath the ocean's surface, like a bubble, and ascended slowly, at an angle, upward and away. Then another emerged, and another, like a trail of balloons, but more precise. They glided up silently and sailed in an orderly procession into the sky, and as they rose they grew larger, one by one growing larger, rounder by degrees as they climbed.

Well, this seemed quite a different kind of marvel, Radu perceived somewhere in the back of his mind, not allowing it to break his concentration. This was different from any past images he'd experienced. It was quite curious. As he watched the procession of moons from the water into the sky, he felt a warming in his center, low in the torso. Gazing inside his own depths with his interior vision he decried a small, glowing figure—like a doll made of light! He shifted his concentration to this miniature light being, and as he watched it broke forth out of the front of his body and moved out onto the waves. The small burning figure traversed the surface of the sea as if it was firm as ice or glass, in the direction of the cross with the moons still ballooning beyond it. Then to his profound amazement, the doll of light with arms extended merged with the cross, and the cross glowed as bright as neon. Radu was flooded with joy, though he could not fathom why—this was all so cryptic, he could not make it out, but he felt it. He felt the joy in every part of his body and he was glad—oh, more than glad, but he knew not words for more than glad, more than joy—

He knew only that he was deeply, and even profoundly, glad and that he did not know why. And he wondered if he could live in that question.

meditation on a sleeping cat

the comfort
of your sleeping breath
teaches me
about trust

the ease
of your body
in that cushion
teaches me
about being

Meditation 18

Shake this heart!
Take my part of this human story
and shout it, ring it in my ears!
Make me hear who I am, what I can
be, free me, with a touch of your hand
on my head, wake me from the dead—

Shake my heart,
Make it start, make it live!
Make it give up its sorrow—
Give in to your love—
Beat through the stone to the light.

The Dark Knight and the Soul

Who is it that disturbs my peace?
Who is it that drapes a heavy cloth over my new
transparent core, my central rodlike clarity?
Who is it that stops up my heart and dims
the light that grew so great within?
Who is it that rattles the old armor, reasserts
its hard doubt, entrenches, digs in?
Whose mailed hand comes before my inner eyes
and masks the holy sight? I am blind.
I am adrift. My new moorings seem unraveling...
I do not feel the tie. I cannot hear Love call.
Who sets me out to sea?

I am the Memory of Fear and Want.
I am the one whom Love abandoned
when I most needed.
I am the one who cried, I am the one who pleaded.
I am the one who resigned all hope...
Who became a stone, turned my mind into a guard,
my heart into a grave. I am the one who forged
the armor you hear clanking over your shoulder.
I want you to wear it again.
I want us to be safe.

From what? What is it we must fight?
What is it we must steel ourselves against?

The world, my friend, the world!
Have you forgot? The world that closes in
and breaks apart. That crushes small things
incidentally, randomly. Then disintegrates
around you, unsubstantial, nothing there.
The world that judges, puts you to the test, the trial,
and finds you lacking. That chooses someone, something
else, leaving you behind. To suffer its inequities,
to never have enough, to never have what you want.
To be passed over, unrecognized, unimportant, ground
down into the dust of disregard. To go unnoticed.
Go on struggling in a life that does not see you,
does not hear you, that does not know you're there
and surely doesn't care.
So you see what this is all about. We must prepare.
We must keep such feelings out. Get dressed.
Put on the metal.

Oh, simple enough, and tempting.
But it will not fit so well anymore. I have grown larger.
Much larger. Except the small, hard ache
that is your domain.
We'd not be contained like the old days. There'd be
parts sticking out. At odds. Divisive. We could not stand.
This well-serviced suit was cast by Defense—my new attire
is fashioned by Desire. Which is stronger? I cannot say.
Except the spinning goes on day by day. A little here
and then a lot. I do not think it can be stopped.
Only arrested—as now.

I think you are deceived.

And I think you have misperceived your purpose
and your stay.
Staunch memory, you squired me well in the days of our

youth. I live and breathe today as proof.
But I am fond to leave the tourney.
It is done. In a strange way I have won.
So. I will to you this sure-struck armor you hold out to me.
It is your battle. Protect your tiny walls, preserve
your little rooms. You are the knight of the child who
lived in the Land of Fear and Want, the Knight of the Small
Dark Place.
I shall ride in my soft raiment, toward the East.
Where the sun lies hidden in a hill.

Meditation 1

I am a Citizen of the Universe.

I am a Seeker of the One Force.

I am a Listener for the One Voice.
And I am an echo of it
resounding, rebounding
back toward the Source.

I am a white bird
in a blue sky
catching the currents.

Soaring high and higher
in the blue, and the blue
becomes lighter and lighter,
until the white bird merges
with the white at the top of the sky.

August 1987

I am on the curve of a small beach; there is a cliff face
before me with several caves in it. As I walk toward the
cliff I see the blue-gowned figure standing in the mouth of
one of the highest caves. I mount a stairway carved into
the cliff wall and enter the cave; I proceed deep into its
interior. At the back of the cave is a colossal light, more
tremendous than anything I have ever witnessed. I see
myself in silhouette against the light, as if I've stepped
back from myself. I watch myself hold up my own heart,
like an offering before the huge light, then I put it inside
my chest...

Returning to the mouth of the cave, I see the figure in blue
inside the opening of another cave. I traverse a narrow
ridge to get to it. I enter; we sit at a table; I ask him: how
can I prevent my thinking mind from interfering with my
search for God? He says: think of God. I smile at the
paradox and the simplicity. Then again I watch myself at
the back of this cave. Again I hold up my hands in an
offertory gesture, but higher and spread apart; within and
above my opened palms something sparkles, like a silver
mist or a cluster of tiny glitterng stars. I am awed and
deeply happy. Then I see myself put also this sparkling air
into my chest. I have a feeling of something tremendous,
something extraordinary. I feel as if I've made some kind
of choice; that I cannot be the same after this...

Meditation 19

We meet on the high road—
the one that defies the mountain side.
We join in the high breeze—
commingle, commune in the still pure
breath of the world where hawks
sail the edges of the sky...

In the high places of the earth,
where clay has been raised up, breathed
into, where scrub and crystal marry the light
and the air—it's there I walk out
to meet the dream of God.

September 1987

I am lying on a raft...gently floating on a large,
undetermined body of water... After some time, I begin
drifting into shore. As I approach, I spy a figure—sitting
on a lone rock at the water's edge. He wears a pale robe,
longish dark hair and close, soft beard. As I disembark
from my raft, he rises and though he does not speak, I
"hear": I have been waiting for you. We stand face to face,
looking at each other intently. As I gaze at him, into him, I
feel something immense, something terrible yet
profoundly serene, rising in me. It is a powerful, awe-full
moment—of recognition—reconciliation. Without
speaking, I "say": I know you are the messiah...He raises
his hands subtly and places them on my head. I continue
to be enrapt in an intense, ineffable sensation... Then he
lowers his hands and we again gaze into each other.
Finally, and still without words, we turn and walk—I
watch as from behind, stationary, as the two figures walk
side by side up the shoreline...

Meditation 20

I leap onto the path like one crazed—
out of my mind—firm, arms flared—
daring!
Dead fast in the middle
of the road—

Do not pass!

Run into me—
Rock me—knock me down!
Press me, till I am not an obstacle
but a cloak, a palm,
laid before your progress...

October 1987

A clear, crystal pyramid suspended in a light blue sky with small white clouds—a human eye in the cone of its top looks directly at me—this remains fixed for some time... Then from a distance above and at an angle, comes gliding down a delicately wrought bronze crucifix and attaches itself to the lower front edge, the base, of the suspended pyramid...

Meditation 21

cathedral oaks,
sycamore and pine,
a sanctuary—

spirit in the leaves,
in the breeze,
turning, touching me—

I bow my head,
rain,
misting, falling,
confirming—

baptism.

Toward a
New Cosmology...
a suite of meditations on
creationism & evolution

Creation I
(meditation 22)

Silent
rolling
fire—

light
expanding,
bursting,
hurling
matter before it—

bang!
hydrogen, helium,
carbon and iron—
bang!
sulfur, cobalt, manganese—
stars and planets and moons...
acid and lightning—
bang!
life—
gurgling, blinking, bubbling life!
swaddled in mud and ammonia...

in the beginning,
in the beginning,
silent, rolling, thunderous Love.

Creation II

(meditation 23)

My mother is Deep Space.

Out of the first folds, sheaths
of light and particle matter, I
plunged—with a tremendous cry!
Parting the membranes of internal,
eternal Memory—coiled, spring
loaded, waiting-wrapped, thrust
by the first birth burst!
Umbilical-propelled, spiraling... spiraling

out... out...

on the rush and gush of Time, expulsed
into the masked and sterile arms of Vast Continuum—
rolling worlds like marbles split by a lightning hit,
scattering stars like diamond chips tossed on a velvet
cloth...

I am imprinted—

as the nautilus bears the Milky Way,
as an atom is a Solar System,
as a handprint blown upon a cavern wall
is the signature of God.

Creation III
(meditation 24)

shell
splitting,
slitting
into continents,
opened muscle
pink
labial

pangaea
cracking,
drifting,
disengaging
in monumental plow —
egg
burst,
enamel and yolk
afloat
on individuating seas —

heart
broken
open
holds the world.

Creation IV

(meditation 25)

Fire and vapor
churning,
mixing,
cooling,
pooling...
methane mud,
microbial mouths
sucking,
sleeping—

vibration
tickling the silt,
God's footfall
wind in the garden,
breath in the leaves—
steaming,
settling,
greening
awake...

And the generations
of Earth were these:
Cyanophyte begat Protozoa
who begat Anemone who begat
Limpet, Whelk and Trilobite
who begat Lacewing Fly

and Pink Flower Mantis
who begat Sea Squirt who
begat Coelacanth who begat
Iguana and Sidewinder
who begat Egret and Eagle
who begat Platypus who begat
Shrew and Sloth who begat
Dolphin, Buffalo, Impala
and Bear, Lemur and Loris
and Macaque...

Love
thrusting into clay,
rising,
dreaming,
aware
and a wonder!

Big Bang?

In the beginning
were Atom and Eros—

matter and love—

neutron notions,
compressed, withheld—
a little proton potion,
a lot of colliding
and riding and writhing—
and those sweaty electrons
dancing and gyrating
and buzzing about—
what could resist?

oh, radiant orgasm
exploding space!
fusion and fission—
ecstatic vision—
eons of neon hot
and aglow
traveling, traveling,
trailing away...slow
and warm
in the arms of deep grace.

Madonna

(meditation 26)

Out of the womb of Midnight Ether:
Art
                    and asteroid—
Beauty
                    and bone—
                                        Compassion
and chromium—
                    Desire
                                        and DNA—
Elegance
                    and elephant—
                                        Fertility
and fire—
                    Geometry
and giraffe—
                                        Heaven
and hyacinth—
                    Identity
                                                            and ice—
Justice
                    and juniper—
Kinship
                    and kidney—
                                        Logos

and lily—
Memory
        and magnet—
Necessity
        and neuron—
                Offering
and orbit—
        Perception
and pear—
        Quantum
                and quasar—
Reverence
        and radium—
Syllogism
        and seagull—
                      Truth
and twilight—
        Union
and umber—
        Vigilance
and velvet worm—
        Wonder
                    and wave—
Yearning
        and yeast—
Zero
        and zygote—

                And God saw
                all that she had made,
                and loved it.
                And therefore
                set it free.

Creation V
(meditation 27)

in the branch,
the bud—
in root,
the seed—
in the limb
needles lengthen,
acorns sleep—

in time,
incarnation

November 1987

I see myself in a small cathedral; I am in the back row, a small, dark figure, seated and still. Then, simultaneously I see myself far forward, before the altar, arms upraised, a celebrant. It is curiously effortless to see myself in both places at once, and seeminly to have even a third position—that from which I view the other two! The scene remains a while... Then my vision fuses, or merges, with the celebrant's, looking upward; for I am seeing the skyward thrust of the sculpted stone and glass. I fall backward slowly, tilting gently back; and as if prone and somehow closer, I see the dome-like structure very near, just above me—as if looking straight on. An odd and beautiful sensation...

A Mass for
a New Age

Kyrie

Lord, come near, be here,
Teach us now, show us how
To have mercy with each other,
To forgive ourselves and one another.
Hear us call—have mercy on us all.

Hear the troubled sigh,
Hear the hungry groan,
Hear the lonely cry,
Hear the homeless moan,
Come near—hear us call,
Have mercy on us all.

Hear the dying cry out,
Christ! Have mercy—
Hear the wretched shout,
Lord! Have mercy—

Have mercy on us who have the means
Yet do not heed these calls—
Open our ears, our eyes, our hands,
Come near, be here—
Have mercy on us all.

Gloria

Glory to God in the stones and the hills,
Glory to God in the trees!
In the fields—in the clouds—
In the rivers and breeze!

Glory to God in the light and the rain,
In the rocks and the caves!
In the creatures of earth and sky,
In the streams and the waves!

The glory of God—is everywhere!
It is there, in the air, in the air
everywhere! Breathe it in, breathe it out,
take it in, send it out, sigh and shout,
sing! Run about—
feel it on your face, in every place!
In your hair, on your hands, everywhere
in the air, it is there!

The glory of God—is all around
in every sound and every shape—
Hold a stone to your ear, you can hear
a star explode—at the beginning—
Take a leaf in your hand, see its grand
design—from the beginning,

when God set the worlds all to spinning!
With a word—it was heard
by all that is, and ever was, and will be...

Listen—to the trees, when the wind
makes them speak, they talk of God—
Listen—to the sea when it swells, it yells, God!
Listen—in the silence, at the center
of the sound—God is heard.
Glory to God in the word...

Credo

I believe in One God!
The Source and Energy of all things!
I believe in the Thought at the beginning of Light!
I believe in Original Sight!

I believe in the Name behind all names!
Yahweh, Brahma, Allah, Jove!
I believe they are each a call
to the Nameless Name behind them all—

I believe the Big Bang was the Great Sound
of God calling Himself into new forms of Being!
God became—light—
God became—the darkness and the waters—
God became—the heavens and the earth—
God became the sun and the planets and the stars!
And God became—one cell—
And became—one fin—
And became—one leg—
One feather. One scale and skin.
And delighted in the multiplicity of eternal possibility!

And God smiled, for it was good To Be anew.

I believe that I am God,
as a baby *is* its mother—
as a baby *is* its father—

I believe that I'm one beam
of an extraordinary blaze!
That furnaces the universe
and fashions all that is—

I believe it's up to me to strike
my soul aglow, to stave off dark,
and to light my way back home...

I believe in the Holy Energy of Christ,
and that it does not leave this world,
for its source did love us so.

Sanctus

Holy... Holy...
Holy is the Spirit...
Sacred, Secret is the Spirit...
Myster and Mother,
You breathed the Word,
Uttered the Sound
that was heard
the world round...

Holy One, One in Three,
Come to us—
Set us free, help us see
Who we are...

Holy...
Holy is the Spirit,
Sacred, Secret is the Spirit!
Wisdom and Grace,
Flow from the stars,
Enter this place!
From the light
and the dark...

Holy One, One in Three,
Enter us—
Set us free, show us how to be
Who we are—

We ask to be filled with the Spirit—
We cry to be full with your Love—
We long to be blessed, to lie down
and rest in the mothering arms of our God...

Benedictus

Wonderous is she,
Honored is he,
Who comes in the Name
Of the Great Energy...

Blessed are we,
Happy are we,
Who gather within
The Great Energy...

Righteous is she,
Noble is he,
Who knows he was born
In the Name of the Lord...

Agnus Dei

Lamb of God,
who blots out
our missings of the mark,
who ignites the spark
that burns us bright,
removes the night
from our sleeping souls,

Awaken us now,
show us how
to be lambs of Your Spirit,
lambs of this world
who walk in your way,
who know the lions' days
are numbered and peace, your peace,
must reign, must reign—
return the dead to the dead,
the living now must free
themselves to be, to be
the Truth—
the lions' days are done,
your gentle victory must be won,
quietly, quietly,
in every heart, in every mind.

This is the start, this is the time.

Salvation

immense love
came
and cried with me,
cracked my heart
and kissed it open,
and we were grateful.

Performance Acknowledgments

Excerpts of *The Debris of The Encounter* have been performed at St. Michael's University Episcopal Church, Unity Church, The Unitarian Society, and Trinity Episcopal Church in Santa Barbara. They are directed by Jan Curtis and feature vocalists Lisa Rutherford, Gary James, Mark Schlenz, Von Gray, Ellen Reidel, Dick Galway, Natalie Beaumont, Alamar Fernandez, Karla Commins, and Jane Hahn. Meditations 5, 7, 8, 18, and "Mass for a New Age" are set for song and speech-choir by Jan Curtis. For information, contact Actors & Playwrights Theatre, P.O. Box 361, Santa Barbara, CA 93102.

"A Mass for a New Age" is set for soprano solo, five instruments, and chorus by composer John Biggs and premiered by the Ventura County Master Chorale under the direction of Burns Taft. For information, contact Consort Press, P.O. Box 50413, Santa Barbara, CA 93150.